Walking on the North York Moors

compiled by
The Ramblers' Association
(North Yorkshire and South Durham Area)

DALESMAN BOOKS
1973

35p.

THE DALESMAN PUBLISHING COMPANY LTD.
CLAPHAM (via Lancaster), YORKSHIRE.
First Published 1973.

Reprinted 1973.

ISBN : O 85206 175 7

The cover illustration of Roseberry Topping is by Bernard Fearnley, and the back cover sketch of Goathland by John Parker. The maps are by R. Gibbs.

Printed in Great Britain by
GEORGE TODD & SON,
Marlborough Street, Whitehaven.

CONTENTS

FOREWORD

ONLY ONE of the walks mentioned in this handy little book is entirely outside the North York Moors National Park boundary — this is the walk in the Lingdale/Kilton area. Concerning all the walks there is a wealth of interest to see, hear, and explore for all ages. I say this because I believe it is the countryside and all the things in it that are important to the walker — not just the problem of getting from point "A" to point "B." Then of course the emphasis changes with the weather, and the weather changes with the seasons, so all in all we have an exciting permutation of landscape, flora and fauna, light and shade, storm and calm, summer and winter, spring and autumn, all waiting to be used and enjoyed, and enjoyed the more by those of us who are not afraid of using our own two feet.

Choose your walk with care — the waterfalls in and around Goathland are much more dramatic on the bright clear morning after the storm when even the tinkling streams are torrents with crests of white foam, and the rivers and fosses are a roar of power and urgency. By contrast is a walk through the stillness of the autumn woods when each crunching step through discarded leaves makes one feel more and more an intruder into this silvan solitude. Take a walk in August over the moor — a sea of unending purple. When with each step clouds of pollen drift away on the silent breeze, hear the honey bees and the red grouse on the peat hagg bidding you "go-back go-back". Come another day to the moor when the wind is strong, and the little pipit or ling lark can scarce make headway as it flits in front of you. If winter is close you might see snow buntings with white wings flashing so much like the snow flakes they herald. See the cliffs in the spring when the shy primroses peep and those denizens of the air, the fulmars, glide and soar around the rocky bastions of our coast. Feel and smell the sea and say "thank goodness I came." Visit Farndale in April and walk through a host of daffodils by the gentle river Dove.

If you should walk such tracks as the drove road or the pannier man's trods, note how countless feet have worn these sandstone paving stones. Think of these folk — their problems and hardships — and make your walk meaningful and enjoyable. If along your way you perchance to meet a farmer, forester, shepherd or gamekeeper, pass the time of day, and remember your full enjoyment depends on good relations between yourself as a visitor and the people whose living is wrought from the fields, the forests, and the moors. No doubt your curiosity has been aroused along your walk; do not hesitate to ask questions for invariably you will find a response and a desire to inform you about the countryside which they so carefully tend.

Lastly, this little book is your key to the pleasures I have mentioned. It has been carefuly compiled by people who have vast experience in rambling, people who derive great satisfaction from walking through the field and forest and over the moor. They wish to enable you to share these pleasures, take a pride in good map reading, remember the safety code and the country code, stick to rights of way which are marked on the definitive map, and above all enjoy your walk.

Richard Bell,
Official Warden,
North York Moors,
National Park.

An invaluable brochure, "Walking over the Moors," is issued by the North York Moors National Park. Further details of the Ramblers' Association may be obtained from 1/4 Crawford Mews, York Place, London W1H 1PT.

TROUTSDALE

Starting Point : In Car Park near Cockmoor Hall, approximately 3 miles to the north of Snainton Village on A.170. Grid Reference 914868.

FROM CAR PARK, follow rough road running east-north east across the cattle grid into Wykeham Forest, and continue for about a mile to join the motor road from Brompton and Sawdon, near a nursery. Follow this road keeping Brompton Moor House on your left, to pass the car park for the Wykeham Forest Trail, and then to pass the fire tower on your right. At the point where the motor road turns south for Wykeham (G.R. 942889) turn left down a steep road, which is rough in places, to cross the Troutsdale Beck and reach the main Troutsdale road.

Turn left along here, and at Troutsdale Low Hall, shortly before the road crosses Freeze Gill, turn left to enter the farm road to Freeze Gill Farm. Behind the farm, the track slants steeply upwards to the right to reach Backleys Farm. Turn left behind the farm, and continue through fields to meet a forestry road. Again turn left to follow this track, ignoring all side-tracks, until at the point where the road turns sharply to the right, Broad Head Farm is reached (G.R. 902881). At this point keep straight ahead on a subsidiary track to descend to the head of Troutsdale. On joining the motor-road, keep forward right to climb the hill back to the car park.

Distance : 8½ miles.

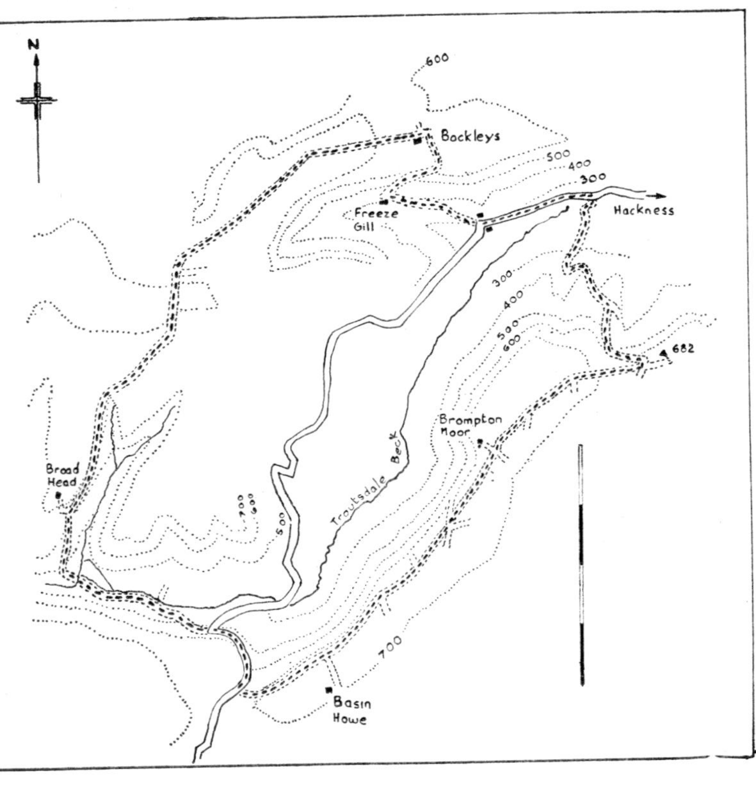
N
600
Backleys
500
400
300
Freeze
Gill
Hackness
300
400
500
600
682
Brompton
Moor
Broad
Head
700
600
500
Troutsdale Beck
700
Basin
Howe

HACKNESS AND BROXA

Starting Point : To west of Hackness Hall in Lowdales Valley at signpost, "Lowdales-Highdales." G.R. 967906.

TAKE THE signposted road, which is both narrow and tarred, as far as Lowdales Farm, the first farm to be reached. Pass between the farmhouse and its buildings, and through a gate on to a farm track up Low Dale and Whisperdale to reach Whisperdale Farm at the head of the valley. Keep the farm on your left and climb up the field to pass through a gate, on the spur between the two minor tributary valleys, into the forest. Continue climbing through the forest, and your path keeps climbing until the summit at Reasty Bank Top is reached (G.R. 964944). There is a car park here, since this point is the start of the Silpho Forest Trails.

Continue by turning left to follow the forest walk westwards along the edge of the northwards - facing escarpment which overlooks Harwood Dale. Follow the track for three miles, half of which is along the escarpment and the other half in dense forest, by means of the "walking man" signs. On reaching farmland, turn left and then right on to Broxa Moor Lane, to make for Broxa village. At start of village, where the main road bears right, bear left. In a short distance, follow a narrow green track between hedges on the left. Follow this until it begins to drop steeply down through a wood when, instead of descending, keep right along the top edge of a wood through several fields for about a mile. The track then crosses to the right-hand side of the ridge, with a small quarry on the left and another wood on the right. At the next gate, a very pleasant track leads down through the wood to join the motor road only a short distance from the starting point.

Distance : 8½ miles.

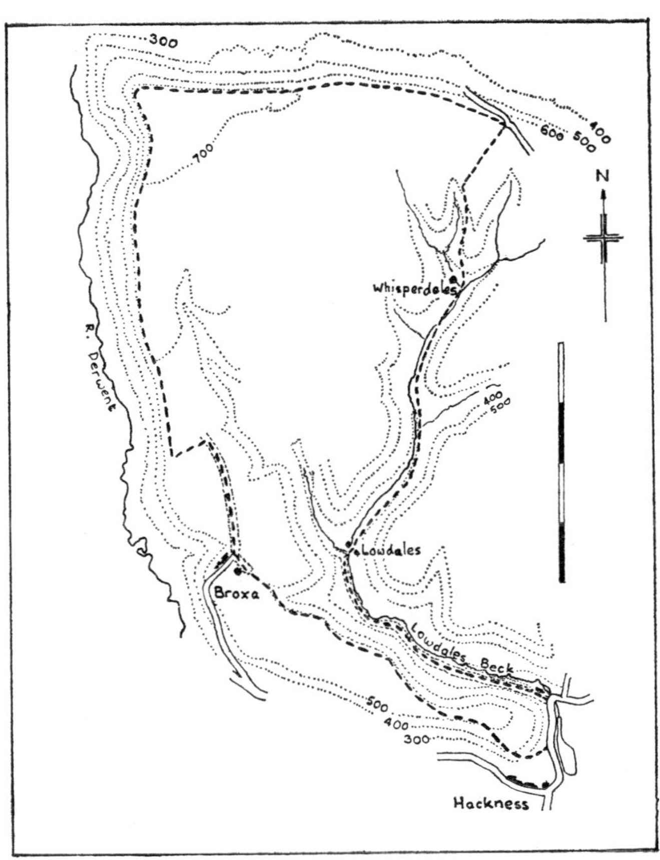
300
700
600
500
400
N
Whisperdales
R. Derwent
400
500
Lowdales
Broxa
Lowdales Beck
500
400
300
Hackness

RAVENSCAR

Starting Point: Adjacent Raven Hall, G.R. 981018.

MAKE FOR the cliff edge, and then turn right to follow the Cleveland Way Coastal Path for 3½ miles to Hayburn Wyke. The final descent from the cliff to the shore can be rather tricky, especially after rain. From the shore climb up the path through the wood, ignoring the Coastal Path signs pointing to the south. Continue up the hill, watching for a path on the right passing over an iron bridge. Go along this path to grid reference 005973 before climbing out of the valley. Follow the track which is parallel to the coast past Plane Tree Farm and White Hall Farm to Prospect Farm (G.R. 998992), where you should turn left to follow the road back to Ravenscar church (G.R. 979012). From here you turn right to return to where you have parked your car.

An alternative short cut is to follow the railway track back from Hayburn Wyke to Ravenscar station, but this route is not dedicated as a right of way.

Distance: 8 miles.

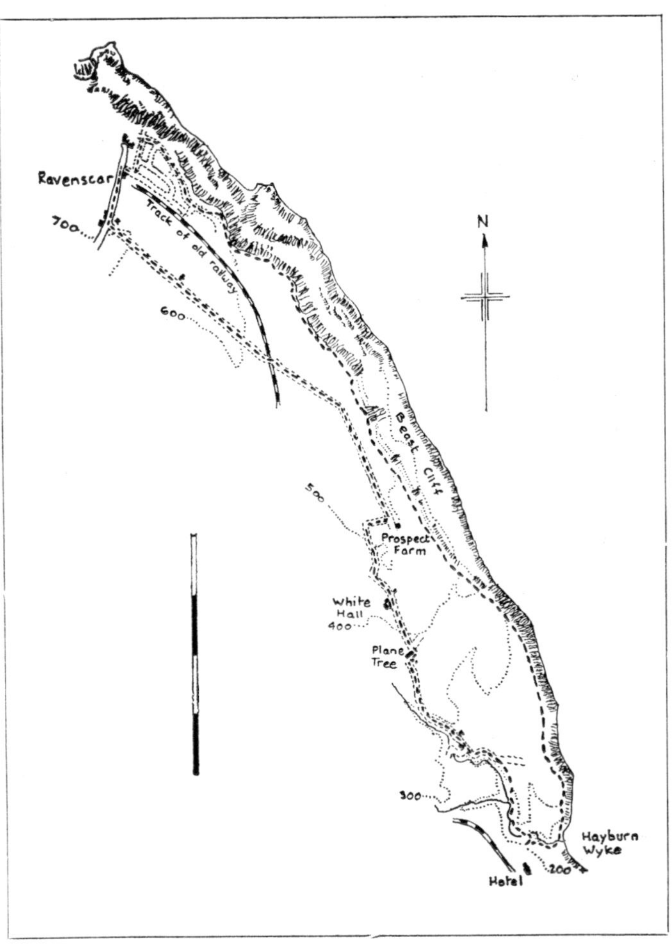
Ravenscar
700
Track of old railway
600
N
Beast Cliff
500
Prospect Farm
White Hall
400
Plane Tree
300
Hayburn Wyke
200
Hotel

HAWSKER BOTTOMS AND THE RIGGS

Starting Point: Whitby Abbey car park, G.R. 904114.

Public Transport: Whitby is served by a rail link with Middlesbrough, and by 'bus services operated by the United Automobile Services from Scarborough, Pickering, Malton, Guisborough, Middlesbrough, Loftus and Redcar.

FROM THE abbey car park make for the cliff edge, and follow the Cleveland Way Coastal Footpath away from Whitby and past Saltwick — once the site of the now defunct alum industry. The fog siren and Whitby Hight Light are prominent features of this magnificent stretch of coastline. Take care when crossing the gullies through which streams reach the sea, since they can be slippery in wet weather. Immediately after passing the third of these (G.R. 941082), past the High Light, turn inland with the footpath signposted "Hawsker." Follow the road through a caravan site, and along a narrow road to meet the Robin Hood's Bay road just short of Hawsker village. In the village cross the main road from Whitby to Scarborough near a chapel. Shortly afterwards the ancient Hawsker Cross can be seen in a garden on the right.

Descend the hill, and near the bottom a stile on the right marks the start of a path crossing the beck. Pass through this stile, cross the beck, and then cross the next large field to another stile. Cross another beck, and keep straight forward to reach Asp House. Cross the road, and pass through a gate along a narrow road. Where this turns sharply left (G.R. 910075), Rigg Mill, now a dwellinghouse, may be seen in the wood below. Continue through the gate down the Riggs to the large house on the left (Golden Grove). Cross the paved yard between the buildings, and proceed down the narrow path past the former Cock Mill. Continue along the flagged path until it reaches the road.

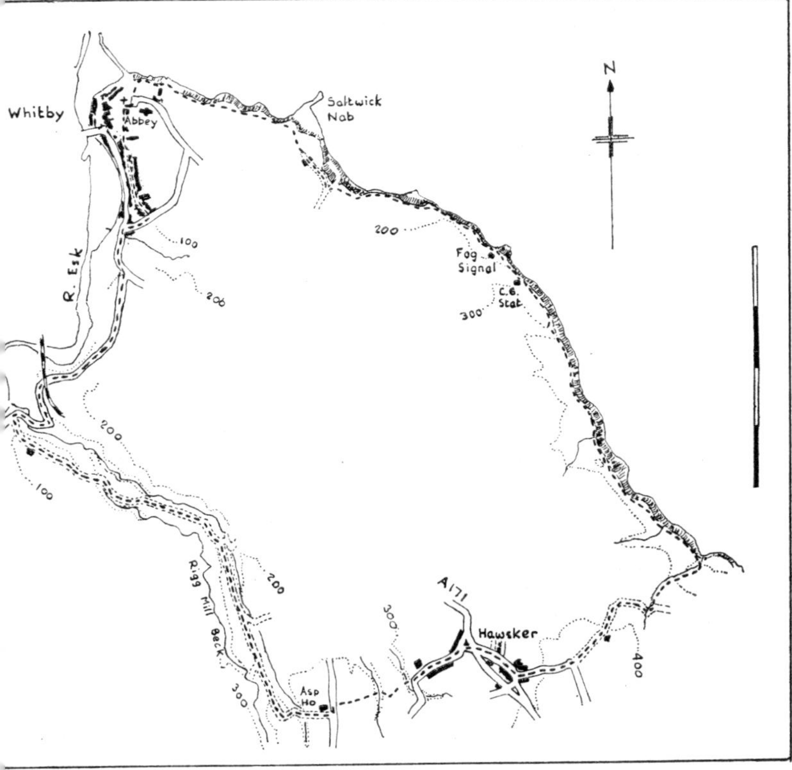

Go straight forward on this road, passing high above the river Esk, before dropping down to harbour level. Green Lane on the right is the motor road back to the starting point. A short distance further along, a steep and narrow paved way (part of an ancient track) leads to a road through a housing estate, and at its northern end becomes a narrow path terminating near to the abbey. An alternative route from the end of Green Lane is to continue along Church Street to the bottom of the 199 steps to the church and abbey.

Distance : 9 miles.

STAITHES CIRCULAR

Starting Point : Car park at the site of the former railway station, G.R. 782186.

Public Transport : The Middlesbrough - Guisborough - Whitby service operated by United Automobile Services passes the junction of the main road with the by-road into Staithes village ¼ mile to the south of the starting point.

DESCEND TO the sea front, and cross the beck to climb the narrow road up to Cowbar village. Follow this unfenced road, first overlooking the cliffs, and then turning inland to reach the main road near Red House Farm. Take the narrow road opposite, and descend into the valley of Easington Beck. Turn left at the road junction beyond the ford and continue along the streamside to Dale House.

The stile in the wall just above the inn is recommended. This takes you over the grassy slope up to the main coast road just to the north side of Seaton Hall. A few yards east of the hall, a signpost and stile take you into the fields on your right and you keep to the top of the valley until you reach a lay-by on the main road close to Hinderwell. Cross over the road and take the signposted path up the rough pasture to Port Mulgrave. Go round below the quarries in a half-circle on the west side.

In Port Mulgrave, turn down the road to the cliff edge and follow the well-trodden path over the Old Nab until you begin to descend towards the coastguard station. Here you leave the cliff edge and take a well-stiled path through the middle of the fields which eventually merges with a very narrow sunken path to St. Peter's church above Staithes harbour. Ascend the narrow winding Slaithes High Street to the cars.

Distance : 6 miles.

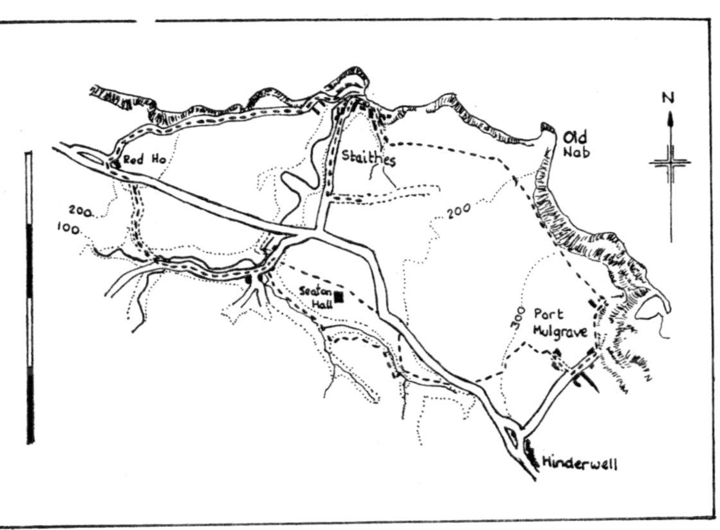
Red Ho
Staithes
Old
Nab
N
200
100
200
Seaton
Hall
300
Port
Mulgrave
Hinderwell

LOFTUS CIRCULAR

Starting Point: Loftus Market Place, G.R. 723182.

Public Transport: Loftus is served by regular 'bus services to Whitby, Guisborough, Middlesbrough, Redcar, Skelton and Saltburn, operated by Saltburn Motor Services and United Automobile Services.

FROM THE Market Place, go down the narrow lane between the Regal cinema and the east end of the church. At the bottom of the hill a footbridge leads you on to a steep enclosed footpath over the new I.C.I. potash railway. Beyond this you make your way in a half-circle to the left, passing the farmstead of South Loftus. You turn through a wicket gate into a broad grass lane, passing a grey tiled cottage on your right. Beyond the cottage you swing left and then right round the head of a valley running down to the main stream below. You keep along the edge of a field, and then pass along an overgrown path between the wood and a high hedge. Turn down to a footbridge at the end of the wood and continue along the edge of the plantation on your right. A stile and signpost mark where you cross the fence into the wood to drop down to the stream side. Keep on upstream until you emerge from the wood into a rough pasture. At the far side of the pasture you turn up to your left and pass through a thicket, and then follow a cart track between the farm and barns of Handale Abbey.

The field road from the abbey takes you to Easington Lane where you turn right until you come to a broad lane leading down past the grounds of Grinkle Park to a footbridge. Climb up the other side of the beck to Ridge Lane and take a path on the other side of the lane to cross Roxby Beck. You leave the wood and make for the farm diagonally left from the stile. Beyond the farm, which you keep on your right, a broad green lane continues as a field road to the inn at Roxby.

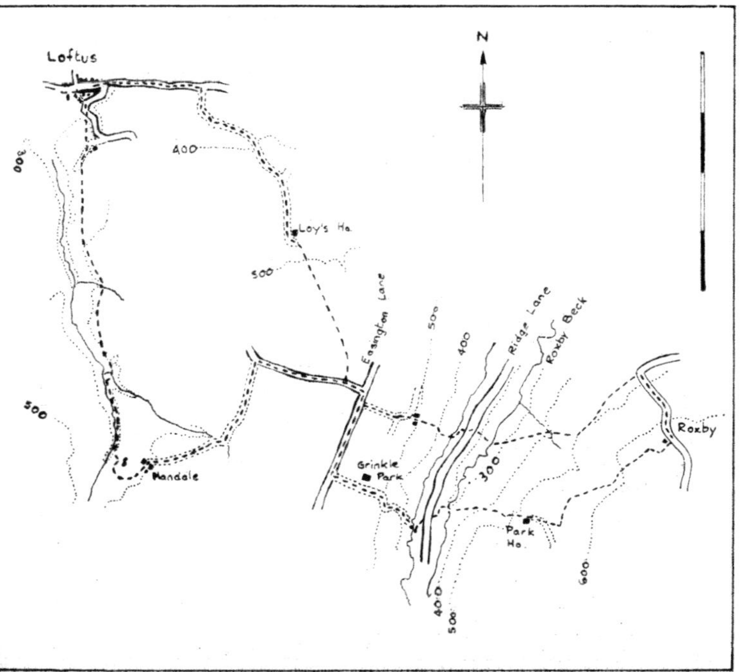

Drop down to the first farm on your left and take a field road on its south side which swings left along a lane into rough pasture. Drop down to a cart bridge at the top of the wood seen below. Then turn south along the open pasture to a stile in the south corner. Cross the stream. Climb up a steep path to the cream-washed cottage where the path goes through the garden between two evergreen hedges. Proceed up the rough road to Easington Lane where you turn right. Then take the first road on your left.

You are now back on the road from Handale Abbey, but you turn down a narrow lane through the woods on your right. This is Loys Lane and it runs back to Loftus cemetery, just below the Market Place.

Distance : 9 miles.

LINGDALE AND LIVERTON

Starting Point : Top of Lingdale village street where roads from Boosbeck, Lower Skelton and Castleton meet at G.R. 675164.

Public Transport : Lingdale is served by the following United 'Bus Routes :— 257/258 : Middlesbrough - Guisborough - Whitby - Scarborough; 259 : Middlesbrough - Guisborough - Danby; 277 : Saltburn - Lingdale; 278 : Redcar (Lakes Estate) — Skelton - Lingdale.

FROM THE CENTRE of the village walk in an easterly direction, with the road to Saltburn and Lower Skelton on your left. Pass the football field and turn right to walk along its eastern edge. Follow a very narrow lane up to the cricket field and from there carry on to Stanghow. Cross straight over the narrow road and take to the fields at a double-gate. Follow the wall on your left and then turn down towards the wood through a wicket-gate. A concrete-stepped path takes you over the valley, and as you climb out of the wood you follow the path below the overhead wires to the Plough Inn at Moorsholm.

Take the north lane out of Moorsholm, and at the first farm on your right turn along the field road opposite. This road swings half-right near Throstle Nest Farm, and reaches a second farm where you turn into the field on the south side of the farmyard. A fairly well-trodden path goes down to Liverton Mill.

Turn up the road to the east, and half-way up the bank take a steep path down to the left. You now follow the Kilton Beck for about three miles downstream to the embankment linking Carlin How and Loftus. Cross this to the west side, and turn back into the woods when you reach the road at the top of some steps above the railway embankment. This path brings you to a substantial bridge below Liverton Mines. You now retrace your way upstream until you reach the confluence of the Hogg and Kilton Becks. There are

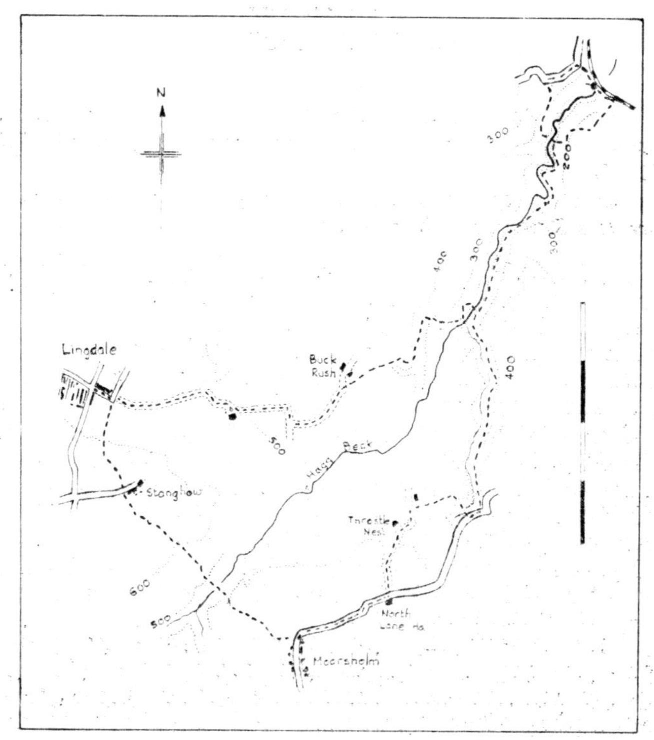

stepping stones here, but they are not very helpful after heavy rain. Take the left fork of the path on the far side of Hogg Beck and work your way diagonally up to the top of the wood. You should come out in the fields near Buck Rush Farm. Just below this farm, there is a field road which takes you back to Lingdale.

One word of caution — many of the land drains which carried water under the path between Liverton Mill and Carlin How have collapsed. In wet weather this route can be very muddy indeed.

Distance : 8 miles.

GOATHLAND

Starting Point: Bus shelter between church and Mallyan Spout Hotel at west end of Goathland's long green, G.R. 828007.

Public Transport: Goathland is served by United Automobile Services Route 91 (Whitby - Malton).

NOT EVERYONE will wish to make a comprehensive tour of all the half-dozen attractive waterfalls within very easy reach of Goathland. This walk will indicate the easiest approaches to the falls, and will also provide the basis for a good day's stroll through some delightful woodland and across stretches of colourful moor.

Start from the Mallyan Spout Hotel by the narrow signposted path from the back of the inn down to the stream. Turn upstream to the west for about a quarter of a mile, and after a scramble over the rocks you will see the mighty cascade of Mallyan Spout dropping over moss-covered cliff on your left. Retrace your steps to the foot of the path from the hotel, and then continue downstream for a hundred yards or so to a stile leading into the fields on your right. Keep along the woodside in a north-westerly direction for three or four fields, and then follow the well-trodden path down a grassy spur to the gaily cream-washed cottages that were formerly Beck Hole station.

Turn north to Beck Hole village. Cross the road bridge near the Birch Hall Hotel. Climb the grassy slope on the right and join a rough road near the railway bridge. Turn sharp right and pass Hill House. A rough track goes due east and follows the tumble-down walls of a few fields. This drops down to Water Ark Foss. There is a bridge at Water Ark and you may cut back to Goathland village by a well-maintained path.

To continue your walk, climb back to the open moor from Water Ark and circle round the north walls of Hawthorn Hill Farm. Beyond the farm drop fairly steeply down to

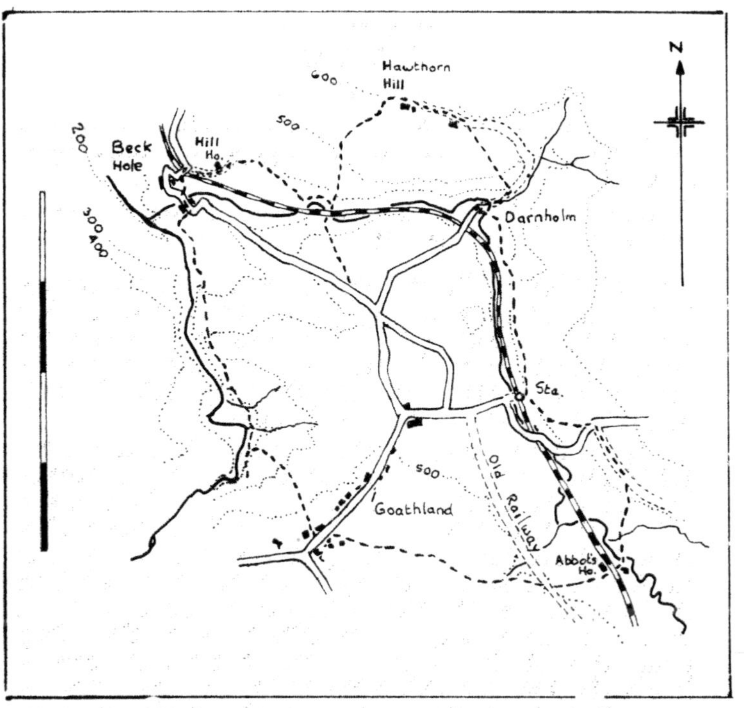

your right to a footbridge near the tumbling rapids and the weir at Darn Holm — a popular picnic spot. From here climb almost due south by the wall-side and walk parallel with the railway track to a point opposite Goathland station. Make your way slightly uphill and cross over the motor road to an open moorland track which takes you to the scattered farmsteads around Abbotts' House. Cross the stream and use the muddy (in wet weather) farm road in a half-circle to the old railway line. Beyond this continue by a field road with the hedge and fence on your left. This takes you back to the church opposite the Mallyan Spout Hotel.

Distance: 5 miles.

GLAISDALE

Starting Point: Adjacent to Glaisdale station, G.R. 784055.
Public Transport: Railway service - Middlesbrough to Whitby.

FROM THE STATION drop down to the white footbridge over the little stream. Climb steeply up the path through the bushes and trees; there should be a signpost "Arncliffe Woods" close to the bridge. The path, paved with large square slabs for considerable stretches, brings you out on to the Egton - Rosedale road. Turn up the hill with Delves Farm House buildings on each side of you. After following this enclosed road for just less than a mile, you reach the open moor. Here you veer to the right, leaving the road and taking a rough track which runs almost due west. Note the prominent tumuli on the left.

After rather more than half a mile you reach a pair of gates in the wall and drop down a sunken rough road to Bank House, from where you turn left and follow the farm track to New House. Turn half left once again along a field road to Low Gill. The route passes in front of this farm-house and continues along the foot of the escarpment to High Gill Farm. A gate on the right, just opposite the stables, takes you on to a track crossing the stream and winding up to Nab End Farm.

Immediately beyond the farm you turn down into the fields, keeping the field wall on your left. Then veer left to a gated footbridge and go straight up to join the "parish road" at Sunnyside House. Turn right and go down the dale back to Glaisdale station. Note that the walk can be halved by crossing the dale from New House to the parish road.

Distance: 8 miles.

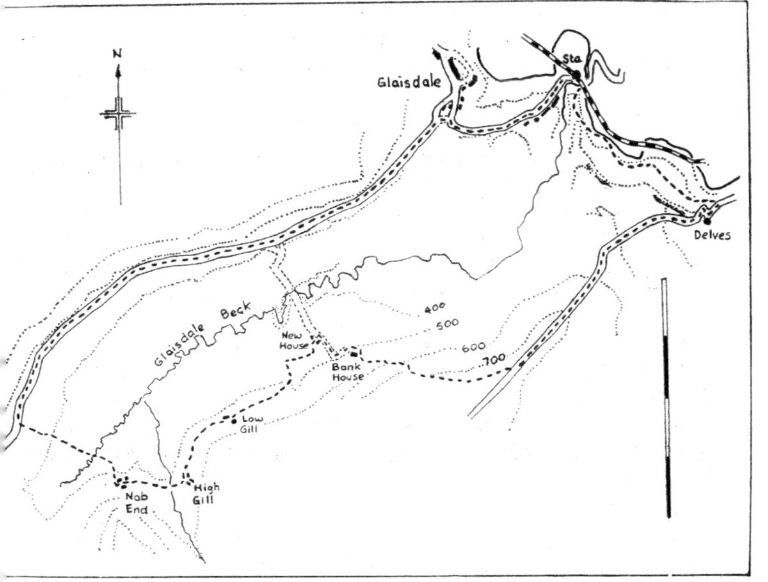

FRYUP DALE

Starting Point: Outside the Fox and Hounds Inn on the southern outskirts of the village of Ainthorpe, G.R. 705076.

Public Transport: The adjoining village of ***Danby is served*** *by United 'bus service from Middlesbrough and also has a station on the Middlesbrough to Whitby railway.*

START NEAR TO the Fox and Hounds Inn, but unless you are a patron do not use the car park. Use some of the waste land adjoining the road to park your car. Carry on up the hill until a sign, "Footpath to Fairy Plain," is reached on the right, just before the road swings to the left. Follow this footpath in a southerly direction, shortly going through a gate. Continue along the track for a mile until just before the descent to the road near Slate Hill House.

From this point there are two alternative routes. You can keep to the track and descend to join the metalled road, keeping to the right to follow a narrow road which climbs the valley side in a south-westerly direction. The other possibility deviates from designated rights-of-way, and follows the contours to join the Fryup — Rosedale road at the top of the bank.

Two-and-a-half miles further on another green metal post marks the turn off to Trough House, a stone shooting lodge. Go eastward for ¾ mile to where a small cairn of stones marks the path which winds down into Fryup Dale. Turn left to follow this path northwards with the dale spread out before you. The path crosses two small streams, then passes through a wooden gate in the stone wall. Follow the path keeping slightly left and continue down the dale, always keeping the wall on your right. Threequarters of a mile further on two wire fences must be climbed before continuing down a grassy path to a narrow metalled road just to the left of Wood End Farm.

Turn left along this road to pass through two gates, ascend a hill and take a right-angle right-hand bend before reaching the more important road. Turn left along this road as far as Slate Hill House from where there is a choice of routes back to Ainthorpe. Either you can follow the metalled road back past Danby Castle, or alternatively you can follow the signposted bridle-road back over Danby Rigg.

Distance : Full walk 8½ miles; walk from Crossley House : 6 miles.

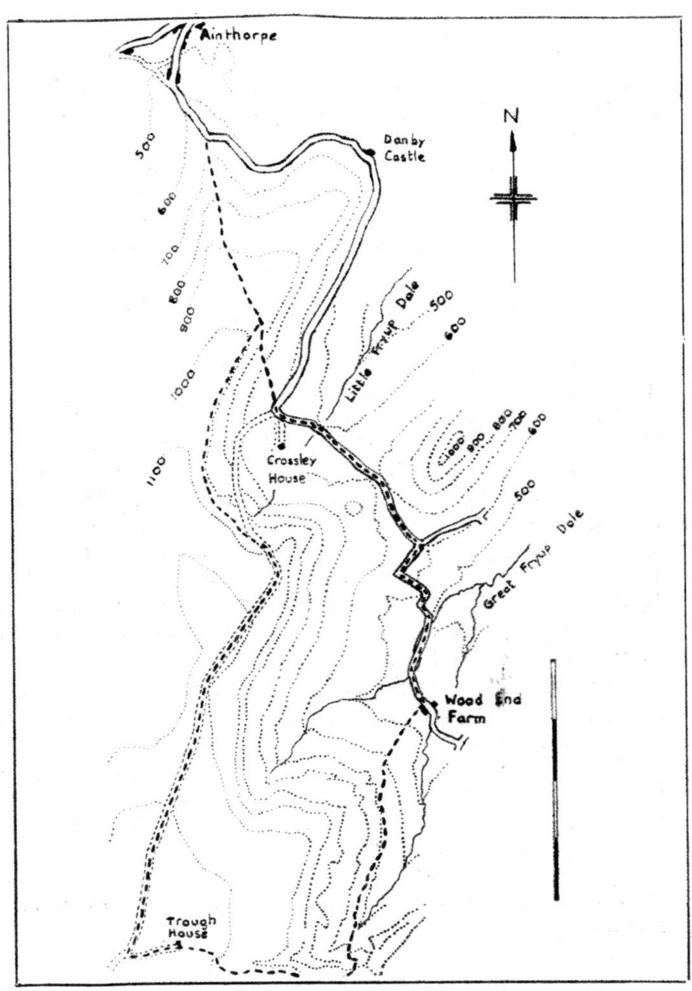

There is no designated right-of-way on a section of the path to the west of Crossley House.

EGTON BANKS AND UPTHORPE

Starting Point: Lay-by on A171 at Barton Howl, G.R. 803083.

Public Transport: This point is served by the Middlesbrough - Whitby - Scarborough 'bus service operated by United Automobile Services.

WALK A short distance along the main road in the Guisborough (West) direction, and bear left on to a minor road. At the crossroads turn left in the direction of Egton to reach the approach road to Moor Side Farm on the right after proceeding a quarter of a mile. Pass in front of the farm buildings, and follow the main track round to the left with marvellous views over to Egton Grange and Glaisdale. At Howe House go through the gate, and then immediately to the right through another gate and across two fields. You reach a wide track passing Westonby House, and continuing to the Glaisdale road.

Turn left on reaching this road, and then turn right in a short distance to follow the farm road down to Thorn Hill. Pass in front of the farm buildings, and follow the grass track down through rough woodland to the footbridge over Stonegate Beck. Ascend to Hall Park Farm, where you should turn left, and at the first gate keep right round the heads of two small valleys. Where the road bears left (G.R. 774078), cross a stile on the right to reach a path to a gate at the top of the field. Turn right along the side of the wall, cross the next field, then keep to the right along fences to reach the Lealholm road at Stonegate (G.R. 774089). For a shorter six mile walk, turn right here and keep straight on to where you have left your car.

To complete the full walk, continue forward along the road opposite with the signpost for Guisborough, to reach the main Whitby - Guisborough Road (A171). Cross it, and go into the farmyard opposite. Pass between the farm buildings,

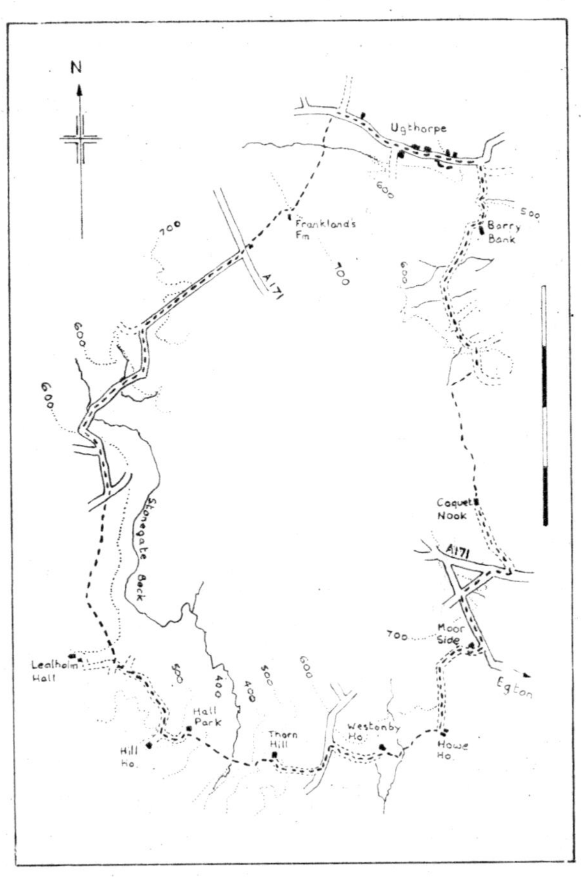
N
Ugthorpe
600
500
Barry
Bank
Frankland's
Fm
700
700
A171
600
600
600
Stonegate Beck
Coquet
Nook
A171
Moor
Side
700
Egton
Lealholm
Hall
500
400
400
500
600
Hall
Park
Hill
Ho.
Thorn
Hill
Westonby
Ho.
Howe
Ho.

and go through the left-hand gate opposite to cross the next field diagonally. Again use the left-hand gate to drop down into the valley, leaving Frankland's Farm on the right. Cross over a stile, turn right and then left at a gate and down two fields. When a short length of track turns left, cross a stile, and from a gate at the top cross a field to the road opposite Ugthorpe mill, now used as a private house. Turn right to walk through Ugthorpe village, and turn right by the church at the far end of the village to follow the road as far as Biggin Houses, in about a mile. Opposite the first of these a gate leads into a field, and so on to the moor. Approaching the highest point, a path will be seen leading left down to Coquet Nook, and so back to the starting point.

Distance : 9 miles.

WESTERDALE

Starting Point : Centre of Westerdale village, G.R. 666058.

LEAVE Westerdale village near the church by a lane proceeding in a south-westerly direction and passing the public convenience on the left. Proceed along this winding road past the youth hostel and the Hall Farm across the river Esk and up to the moor edge. Go through a gate, and turn left along the road to New House. At the bend just before the farm, pass through the second of two gates on the left to cross the field diagonally to the white gate at the far end. Keep the river on your left, cross Stockdale Beck by a white

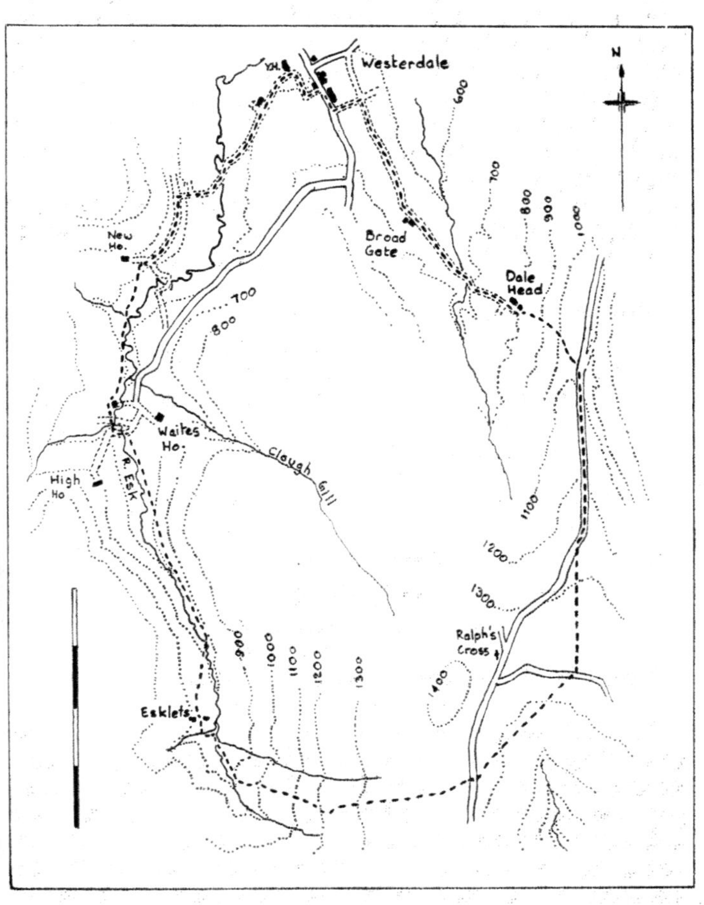
Westerdale
Y.H.
N
600
700
800
900
1000
New Ho.
Broad Gate
Dale Head
700
800
Waites Ho.
Clough Gill
High Ho
R. Esk
1100
1200
1300
Ralph's Cross
900
1000
1100
1200
1300
1400
Esklets

foot bridge, and continue to a stile in the wall. Keep above the river over a stone step stile to the left of a telegraph pole. At Wood End Farm go through a metal gate on the right and behind the farm, then through the gate of the stack yard and over the stone step stile. Continue over the metal foot bridge, cross the next field and then left to reach and cross the black and white metal foot bridge near the ford.

Turn right and follow the river upstream across three fields. At a boggy patch where the river is joined by a tributary stream, turn uphill for 25-30 yards to meet the green path from Waites House Farm. The path is well-defined, and passes through bracken as valley narrows. Cross the stream by a foot bridge and continue to the ruined farm-house of Esklets. Go through the buildings to find an enclosed lane leading to a stream-bridge. Then follow the Lyke Wake Walk white posts left to cross the stream and climb up the moor, to reach the Blakey Ridge road adjacent to the Margery Bradley Stone. A faint track leads over the head of Rosedale to reach the Castleton - Rosedale Road at White Cross (sometimes known as Fat Betty). It is possible to turn left on reaching Blakey Ridge road and then to turn right into the Castleton - Rosedale road to reach White Cross.

From White Cross follow the parish boundary stones to reach the Castleton Rigg road half a mile to the north. Continue forward along the road for a further threequarters of a mile until you reach the point where it forks right to descend into Danby Dale. From this point follow a faint track which descends to the left, across the moor to Dale Head Farm. Keep to the left of the farm and continue with the wall on your left. Descend to cross Tower Beck and follow the track past Broad Gate Farm to reach the cross-roads, where you should turn left into Westerdale village.

Distance : 10 miles.

ROSEBERRY TOPPING AND EASBY MOOR

Starting Point: Ayton High Green on the secondary road through the village of Great Ayton, G.R. 563108.

Public Transport: At the time of writing this walk is suitable for the non-car owner, since Great Ayton is served by the following United 'Bus Services:—280/281: Stokesley - Guisborough - Redcar; 290: Great Broughton - Stokesley - Middlesbrough.

LEAVE Ayton High Green in an easterly direction (left if standing facing the school), and then turn left into Newton road. Cross the road to an iron gate in the wall on the right-hand side. Pass through the gate and follow a well-marked footpath through fields with Cleveland Lodge on the left. The path crosses the railway by a line-side cottage and in a short distance a sharp turn right leads you diagonally upwards in a north-westerly direction to Cliff Ridge Wood. Through this you climb diagonally to the right to a stile at the far edge, from where you cross the field towards the gate on the left to Airy Holme Farm. Keep the farm on the right, and pass through another gate on to a cart track, which will ultimately be seen leading up to the summit of Roseberry Topping. It is a little over half-a-mile from Airy Holme Farm to the base of this peak.

From the summit of Roseberry Topping, descend eastwards by a well-defined path to the col which separates this eminence from the main ridge of the Cleveland Hills. Beyond is Newton Moor. Follow this path along the escarpment towards Gribdale keeping the wall on the right. In about two miles from Roseberry Topping you cross a minor road, and ascend by the track opposite to Captain Cook's Monument on the summit of Easby Moor.

After reading the inscription on the base of the monument, descent by a well-worn track leading in a north-westerly direction to a wood on the left. This track is approximately

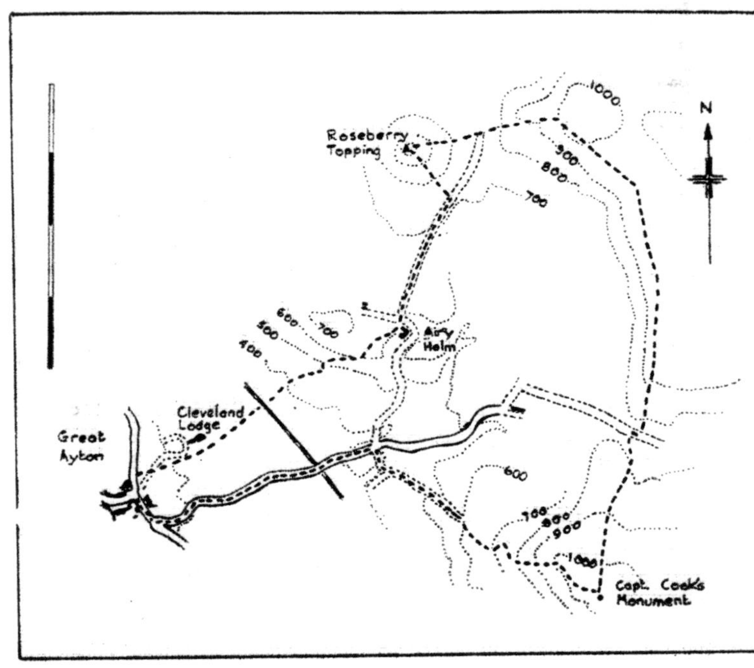

at right-angles to the one used to ascend Easby Moor. Ultimately, near the base of the main ridge, it is joined by another path coming in from the left, and soon becomes a lane leading down to a cross-roads. Turn left at the cross-roads, and follow the lane down past the railway station into Great Ayton village. At the T-junction on the outskirts of the village turn right, and in less than a quarter-of-a-mile you will reach the High Green.

Distance : 8 miles.

EASTWARDS FROM CLAY BANK

Starting Point: On B1257 (Stokesley - Helmsley) at the summit of Clay Bank, G.R. 572035.

Bus Service: At the time of writing this walk is also suitable for the non-motorist, since the 292 'bus route (Middlesbrough-Helmsley) passes the starting point.

FROM THE CAR PARK at Clay Bank summit walk along the main road towards Helmsley and Chop Gate for about 150 yards, then pass through a gate on your left with the L.W.W. sign on the post. Your path follows the wall on the left and climbs up through a rocky "gorge"to come out on the moor. Just through the gap where a gate should be, and almost at the highest point on the moor, a track turns off to the right from the main path, leading to and then following a deep ditch with a mound shown on the map as "earthworks."

Follow the path across the moor: it crosses a beck then breaks back on itself on the other side. As you continue turn round to look through the gap in the ridge at both Roseberry Topping and Easby Moor crowned by Captain Cook's Monument and framed by the Cleveland Hills — a truly wonderful sight. The path and ditch bear left and climb slightly on to level moorland. Cross two further small streams, whereupon the ditch disappears and is replaced by a dry stone wall. Follow this wall to its end — it turns down to your right. The path can be seen to continue on to cross a rather wet patch and reach the bridle road which has ascended from Chop Gate and Seave Green.

Turn left here (there is a large notice-board erected by the Feversham Estates about the use of moor tracks, etc.), and climb on the bridle road to the moor where another small signpost says "to Bloworth Crossing." Continue along this track which is a fire-break made on the lines of the path. This continues for about a mile-and-a-half, until it meets a track of similar size at a T-junction. There is a cairn on

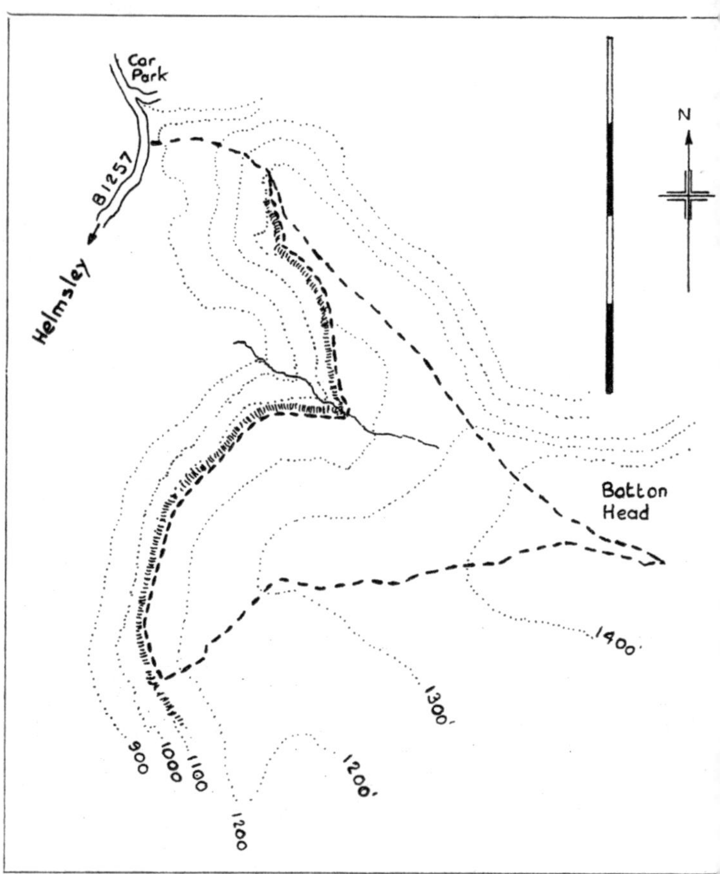

your left, and on the moor in front on the other side of the track is the trig point on Botton Head, the highest point on the North York Moors at 1,489 feet above sea level.

Turn left along this track, and follow it all the way back to the car-park at Clay Bank. This route from Botton Head is that of both the Cleveland Way and the Lyke Wake Walk.

Distance : 6 miles.

CHOP GATE, CARLTON MOOR AND COLD MOOR

Starting Point: Public car park adjacent to the Women's Institute immediately to the south of Chop Gate village, G.R. 558993.

Public Transport: Chop Gate is served by the United Automobile Services Route 292, Middlesbrough to Helmsley.

TAKE THE rough track up the steep hill until it eventually peters out. Then follow a deep dry gully straight up the hillside. There is no clear track, but the right of way runs just to the south of the crest of the long spur of the hill known as Trennet Bank. There is a good half mile of gentle climb to the tumuli and boundary stones on the highest point of the moor where you turn north by west. The route follows a line of prominent mounds and boundary stones till you reach a metalled road. This drops gently down to a point where an electric overhead cable crosses a col between Carlton Moor and Trennet Bank.

The road drops down to the east at this point, but you must keep ahead through a narrow cleft in the rocks and continue north-west. Keep the highest point of the broad ridge on your right and after half-a-mile you will see the "hide" near Brian's Pond. This lies on the west side of the path. Beyond the pond you go due north passing two sets of rocky outcrops to reach the bare glider field on Carlton Moor. Keep well to the eastern edge of this and you will strike a well-worn sheep track through the heather and bracken to join the broad bull-dozed road used by the gliding club's vehicles.

Follow this road down to the Carlton to Chop Gate motor road. Cross over this road and make your way along a well-used track over Cringle Moor. Alternatively, there is a more sheltered track well below the top of Cringle Moor on the north shoulder. Both tracks bring you to the pass

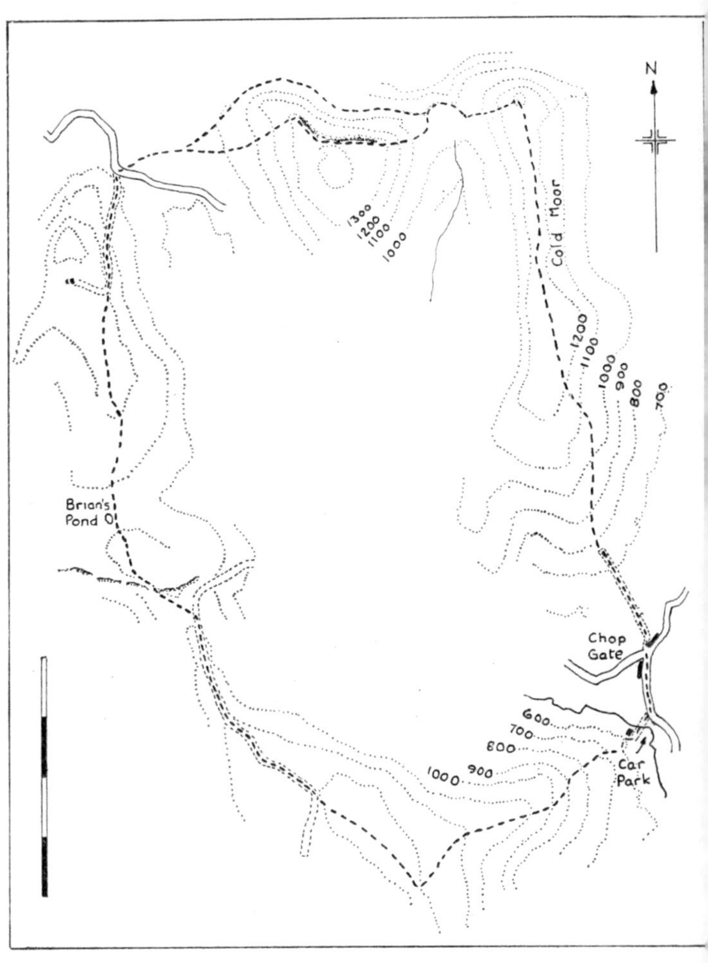

The alternative northern path at the upper edge of this map is not a designated right-of-way.

between Cold and Cringle Moor. Make your way up to the crest of Cold Moor where the track due south is clearly bulldozed for quite a considerable distance. Keep along the crest of the ridge to a group of tumuli. There are few signs of a track beyond this, but the direction of the bridle-track on the one-inch map is south-eastward, gently diagonally descending the flank of Cold Moor. After about a mile-and-a-half you will come to a gate in an angle of the wall, where you join a narrow overgrown lane running down into Chop Gate.

Distance : 9 miles.

SWAINBY CIRCULAR

Starting Point : Adjacent Swainby village church, G.R. 478020.

Public Transport : Swainby is served by 'buses operated by the United Automobile Services from Middlesbrough, Stockton-on-Tees, Stokesley and Northallerton.

FOLLOW THE ROAD south towards the hills until you reach a left-fork signposted to Scugdale. Take this road for about half-a-mile until you reach the hamlet of Hushwaite Green, where there is a telephone box and a broad track crossing the road. Turn left through the gate to join the Lyke Wake Walk and the Cleveland Way, distinguishable by the white acorn sign. The broad track climbs steadily

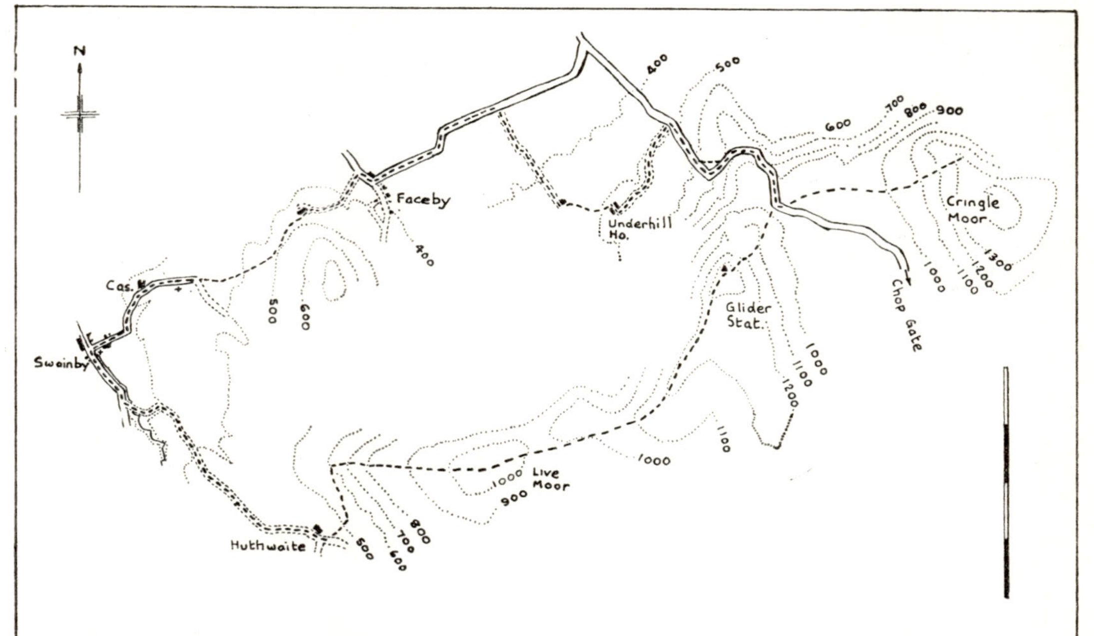

There is no designated right-of-way on a section of the path to the west of Underhill House.

upwards with forestry on your right and, on a clear day, extensive views westwards to the Pennines. Still climbing the path bears to the right and comes out on to the open moorland, going up the northern flanks of Live Moor and Holey Moor ultimately to reach the top of Carlton Bank with its flat surfaced area and hut of the Teesside and Newcastle Gliding Club. The track now drops steeply to the Chop Gate — Carlton road.

From the road, the large hill ahead is Cringle Moor (1,427 feet), and for those people wanting an extension, is worth climbing. Otherwise turn left along the road which drops steeply downhill round an S-bend, the second corner of which can be cut off. About a quarter-of-a-mile past this corner, a lane leads off on your left to Underhill House. Your route leads through the farmyard and from the far right-hand corner crosses the field to a point about 200 yards from the top edge, where you cross into the next field. From here, bearing slightly to the right, you cross diagonally towards the nearest farm. You pass this farm and follow a good track down to the Carlton — Faceby road. Turn left here and follow the road to Faceby village.

The road turns right here and after a short distance you take a road on your left leading uphill. You pass a factory farm on your left, after which the road becomes a rough track. You have a wooded hillside on your left and you should be careful on reaching the end of this not to take the left-hand path leading uphill on to the moor. A lower path leads through a gate and keeps on the right-hand side of the hedge. The path is now fairly obvious and leads downhill to the remains of Whorlton church, which is worth a visit. On your right are the remains of Whorlton Castle. About half-a-mile along the road and you are back in Swainby village.

Distance : 9 miles (11 miles including Cringle Moor).

N.B.: The section of this walk immediately west of Underhill House is not a designated right-of-way.

BLACK HAMBLETON

Starting Point: On minor road between Osmotherley and Hawnby, 2 miles from Osmotherley on the top of the moors where the road makes a left-hand right-angle bend before descending into Ryedale. G.R. 479959.

THE WALK STARTS by following the Cleveland Way southward from the starting point, the route being clearly marked by the white-acorn sign used by the Countryside Commission to denote long-distance footpaths. Furthermore if you approach the start from Osmotherly, the route is easily distinguishable as the track continuing straight on as the road bends to the left.

Follow the long-distance footpath (the Cleveland Way) to the foot of Black Hambleton where coniferous forest is to be found on your right. Take the second gate into the forest which you will find is signposted "Footpath to Nether Silton." Initially this is a green and rather pleasant grassy track, but soon becomes a forestry road with the typical black unmetalled surface as it descends into the valley. Before the track levels out, pass two forester's huts, and continue straight ahead through the gate leading out of the bottom of the forest.

Approximately half-way between this gate and the farm (Hunter's Hill) the road passes over a stream, about fifty yards beyond which is a caravan and two gates. Take the second of these gates, and keep to the left-side of two fields until you pass through a wooden gate at the end of the second one. Turn right towards another gate beside a hollow tree stump. Go through this gate and walk to end of field, where you should turn right until you come to and cross a stile by a large tree.

Walk diagonally across this field, keeping Honey Kiln Farm on your right and Thwaites Farm on your left, to reach the track by the gate leading to Thwaites Farm. Cross the fence to the track, and cross the fence immediately opposite with

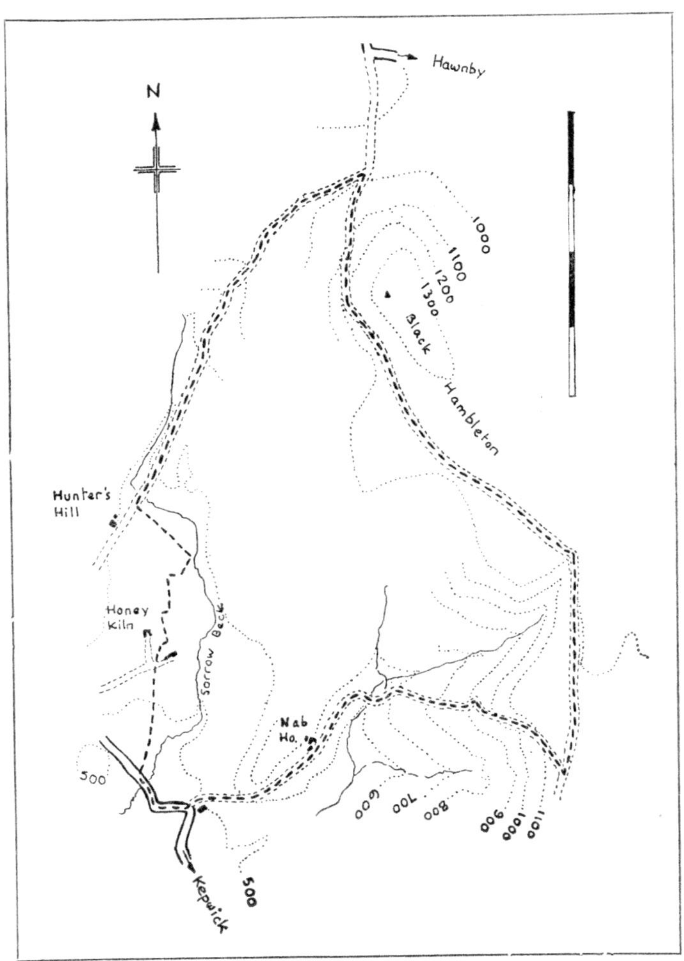
Hawnby
N
1000
1100
1200
1300
Black
Hambleton
Hunter's
Hill
Honey
Kiln
Sorrow Beck
Nab
Ho.
500
600
700
800
900
1000
1100
500
Kepwick

field boundary on your left. Carry on through this field towards the gate at the bottom left-hand corner, and then downhill to another gate at left-hand corner of next field. After passing through this gate, keep well to left of field to cross the fence at the bottom. Follow the boundary of the last field round to the right to pass through a white gate on to the lane leading from Nether Silton to Kepwick.

Turn left along the road, and follow it for quarter of a mile until a stone house is reached on the left. Leave the road by taking a track immediately before this house and passing through a white gate marked Nab Farm. Follow the track, through a gate and over the adjoining cattle grid and when the farm is reached pass through a gate on the right which keeps you to the right of the farm buildings.

Follow the track down to the stream coming from Black Hambleton. Cross over the stream, and take track to the left which leads past an old kiln, after going through a gate. You are now in open country, and should follow the track as it winds up towards a stone wall. As you ascend keep parallel with this wall, ignoring any deviation the track might appear to make on the left. You will join a wider track again further up the hillside. Note the rocks up the hillside on the left: Whitestone Scar. Almost at the end of your climb pass through a gate onto a broad grassy track, the Cleveland Way.

It is worthwhile at this point turning back to look where you have come from. Immediately below you is Nab Farm, almost looking like a miniature doll's house, and beyond it the Vale of Mowbray is spread like a carpet to the Pennines in central Yorkshire. The great vale stretching in front of you to the horizon is Wensleydale, and the prominent peak immediately to the left is Penhill.

Turn left after passing through the gate, to follow this ancient drove road and new long-distance footpath back to the starting point. Remember to take the left-fork in three-quarters of a mile at the brow of Black Hambleton, and in due course you will see your car down below in front of you. As you descend, note Osmotherley village and church behind some small reservoirs slightly to the left in front of you.

Distance : 8 miles.

PARADISE

Starting Point : On minor road between Boltby and Hawnby, 1 mile from Boltby, 25 yards up Sneck Yate Bank where well-defined forestry track goes off to left and there is a wide-enough open space to park your car. G.R. 503872.

PASS THROUGH the gate by which you have parked your car, and follow the forestry track, passing on the right after about a mile the Ryedale Water Boards Reservoir. Proceed along the path, straight on at first, and then turn right at the second junction. Turn left at the next junction, and then at the top of a small incline turn right by a fire precaution sign. Climb small hill to a cross-roads, cross over and ascend to the main ridge of the Hambleton Hills by a long sloping track. There are excellent views on your right of the remainder of the Paradise Valley and of the Vale of York to the hills of the West Riding.

At the broad track at the top of this hill, turn left and then right to follow a rather muddy track to meet the drove road and the Cleveland Way at the top, where you turn right. Continue along the unmetalled drove road, through a gate at the end of the forest, to reach a gate on the right-hand side, signposted "Moors Path" and leading to High Paradise Farm. Follow farm track through High Paradise to a bend in the road just past the farm gate. Then continue on broad green track on left through three gates to reach metalled road near top of Sneck Yate Bank. Those people wishing to follow the shorter route can descend the Bank back to their cars.

Those wishing to follow the longer route should cross the road to the High Barn farm gate, pass through it and follow the track to the farm buildings on top of the hill. Turn sharp right just past the buildings, and descend the hill by a broad green path, turning left at the wall and passing through a gate at the end of a wire fence. Head down hill to a sunken track bordered by bushes, and turning right follow a wire

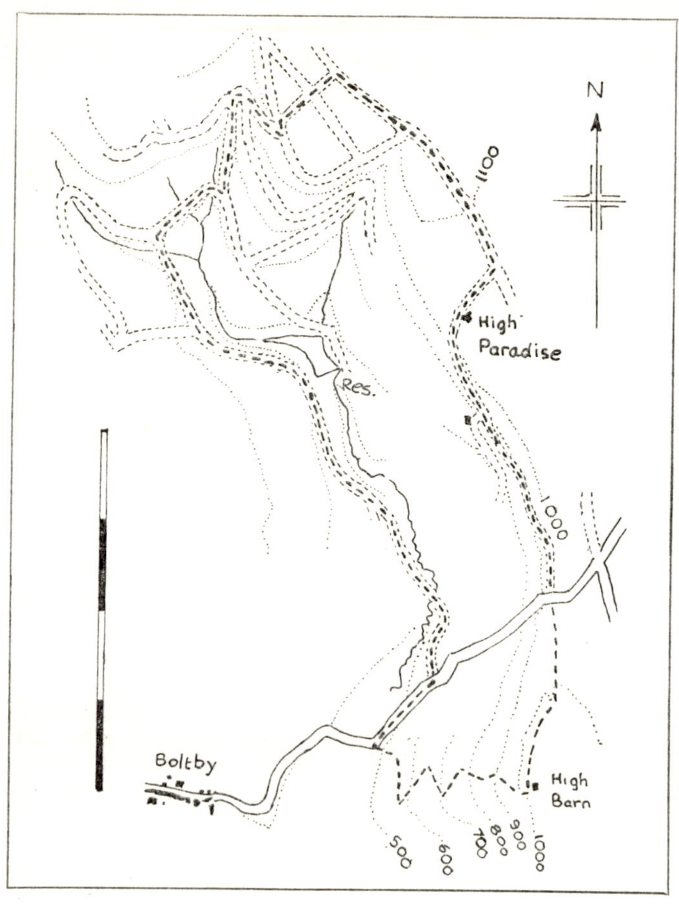

fence down to a forestry track. Turn right on this track and follow it out on to the road. Turn right on road and return to car in short distance.

Distance : 8½ miles (full route); 5½ miles (shorter route).

WHITE HORSE OF KILBURN

Starting Point: Car park at the summit of Sutton Bank on the Thirsk - Helmsley road (A170) four miles from Thirsk, G.R. 514830.

Public Transport: This point is served by the United route from Ripon and Thirsk to Helmsley.

START THE WALK by following the footpath which joins the main road from the south, almost opposite the junction with the by-road to Cold Kirby and Old Byland The path continues along the top of the ridge for a mile-and-a-quarter, with the steep escarpment on the right and, after the moors path has turned off to the left, the premises of the Yorkshire Gliding Club on the left. At the end of the path you will reach the White Horse, identifiable at this stage only as a large white area immediately below on the right from which both turf and vegetation have been cleared.

Immediately beyond this descend the hillside by a series of steps to a car park clearly visible below on the right. Continue descending the hillside by the minor road, by a series of hairpin bends, until just after passing the steep hill sign erected for the benefit of ascending motorists. Immediately beyond this follow the rough road branching off to the right and, where it turns left to Acre House Farm, keep straight on along a grassy track between hedges, ultimately passing through a gate into a forestry plantation. Follow the track into the Forestry Commission land, avoiding a grass track forking off to the left, until the main access track comes in from the right.

Keep straight on along this track to take the left fork at the bottom of the hill. Your way winds round the side of Hood Hill, and as the path bears left the boundary fence is immediately on your right. As soon as the boundary fence moves away from the track, follow the fence downhill to pass through a wicket-gate into a field. Walk down the field towards Hood Grange (the ancient stone farmhouse, a quarter of a mile away in the valley bottom). Before reaching the farm turn left along the field boundary, which should be followed round to the right, with the farmhouse on your right, until you reach the metalled road by the farm gate. Turn left along the access road, and follow it round a right and left-hand bend until the main Thirsk - Helmsley road is reached.

Turn sharp right on to the main road and at the top of a short incline, in about a hundred yards, turn left to follow the access road to Cleaves Farm. On gaining the farm buildings pass through the gate in front of you at the far end, and follow the rough track across the field and through another gate. In front will be seen a third gate. Do not go through this, but bear slightly to the left, and follow the hedge towards a fourth gate between some small trees. The way is now clear to Cleaves House, a group of farm buildings in front, and with a large gate filling the gap between them. Pass through this gate and turn right along the minor road.

In a quarter of a mile a cottage with elegantly cut yew trees is reached on the left, and notices proclaim that you have reached the end of vehicular access. Bear slightly right immediately after passing the cottage and enter the Yorkshire Naturalists' Trust's Garbutt Wood Reserve. In about one hundred yards from the cottage a narrow path will be seen bearing left as the main path bears right. It is signposted "Thirlby Bridle-Path." Follow it gradually uphill; there are a number of deviations, but provided you always choose one which ascends the top will obviously be reached. At the highest point the Cleveland Way is reached as it follows the escarpment edge from Sneck Yate Bank to Sutton Bank. Turn right and in three-quarters of a mile you will have returned to the car park whence you started out.

Distance : 7 miles.

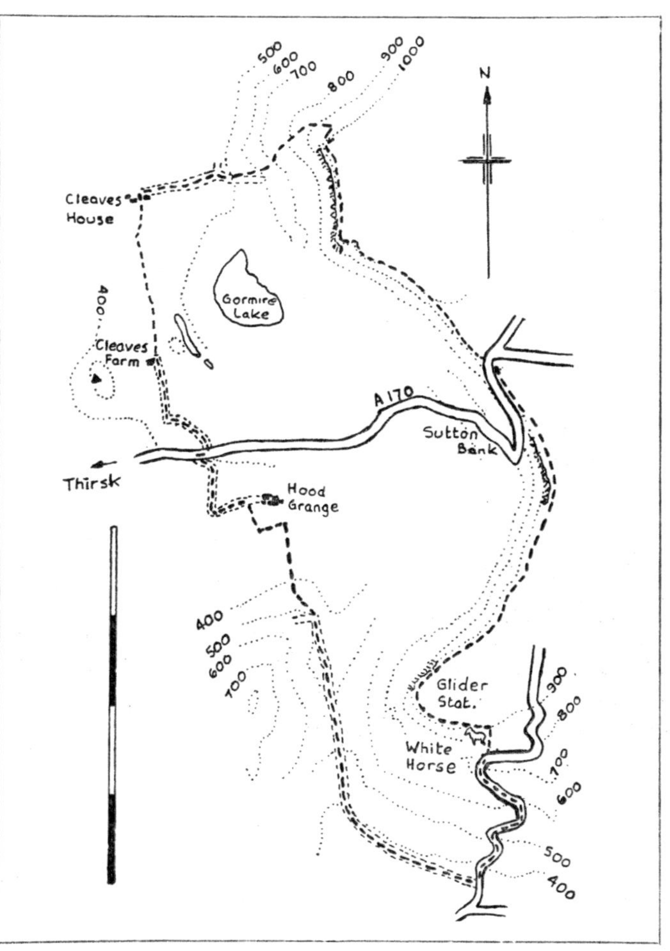
500
600
700
800
900
1000
N
Cleaves House
400
Gormire Lake
Cleaves Farm
A 170
Sutton Bank
Thirsk
Hood Grange
400
500
600
700
Glider Stat.
900
800
White Horse
700
600
500
400

RYEDALE
including Shaken Bridge and Rievaulx

Starting Point: Newgate Bank Top car park, G.R. 563890.

Public Transport: This point is served by the United Automobile Services route 292, Middlesbrough - Helmsley.

GO TO THE south-west corner of the car park and use the forestry gate or stile leading on to a broad ride. This slips gently down for half-a-mile. Then turn back sharply to the left, that is south-west, along the edge of a fenced plantation to a white gate. Still descending, turn sharp right to the thatched house, Broadway Foot.

Turn sharply back south and look out for a wicket gate into the wood on your right. The first little gate is "Private"; you use the second gate. Drop down through the bushes to the road near Shaken Bridge, and follow the road to the farm on the other side of the Rye. Climb up the farm road to the top of the slope, and follow it along the edge of the wood. You pass a ruined farmhouse and continue along a rough field-track to reach a broad pasture overlooking a new bungalow in the farmyard of Barnclose House. Drop down over an open pasture to a gate and take the sunken lane on the south side of the farm to the bridge below Tylas House.

Follow the field road over the shoulder of the hill beyond Tylas House, and as you drop down into the valley look out for a dilapidated stile just over a little stream. This leads into the fields on your left. Cross the field to a clump of trees close to the riverside in the extreme southern corner of the field. You work your way along a rather precipitous stretch of path among the trees overhanging the rushing river Rye. Beyond the wood, a stile in a wire fence leads across a drainage ditch. Turn south along the edge of the plough and the foot of the rough pasture hillside on your right. At the far end of this field you meet a narrow road, which comes up from the Bow Bridge over the Rye.

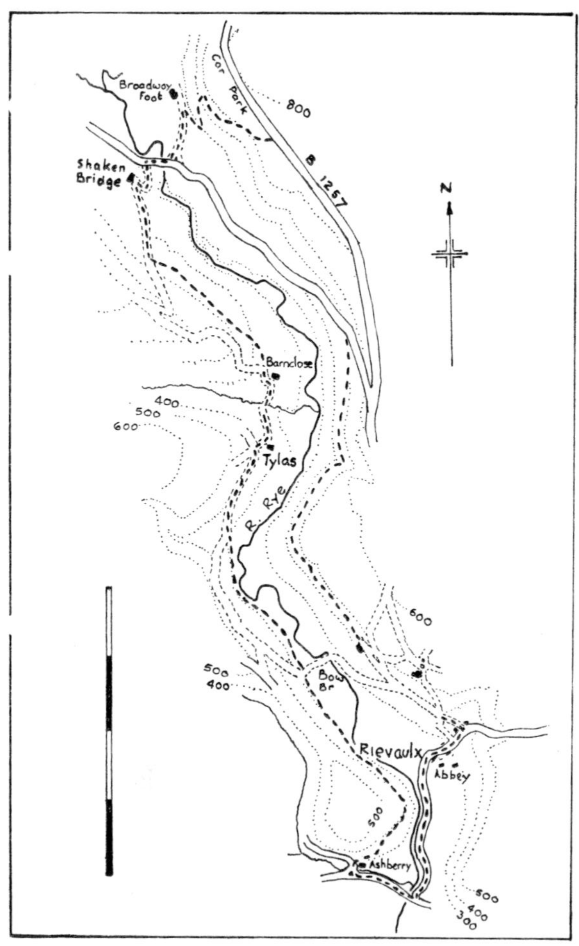

There is no designated right-of-way on the path from Rievaulx to the Hawnby-Helmsley road.

Cross this road to a field gate and take the track across the fields leading up into the wood on your right after three fields. Continue along the woodland track down to Ashberry Farm. Cross the roadbridge and take two left turns to Rievaulx Abbey.

Keep along the road winding round past the abbey into Rievaulx village, and just below the woods on the hillside turn off along a narrow road to the left, passing the Wesleyan methodist chapel. Keep straight along this terraced walk through Hagg Woods till you reach Hawnby - Helmsley road. Turn up to your right, and then take the first turn left along a broad forestry ride which brings you back to the thatched farmhouse at Broadway Foot. From here return to the car park via the same route as on the outward journey.

Distance : 6 miles.

RIEVAULX ABBEY CIRCULAR

Starting Point : The car park adjoining Rievaulx Abbey in the village of the same name, 2 miles west of Helmsley, G.R. 575850.

Public Transport : The Middlesbrough - Helmsley 'bus service passes along the main road half-a-mile to the east of Rievaulx village.

IT IS particularly recommended that this walk be done in springtime or winter when certain woodland paths are more easily negotiated in the absence of undergrowth.

On leaving the car park turn right up the hill towards the church. Go left on the road opposite the church, passing the methodist church on your right and a large new house on your left. Where the road forks take the left road through a gate down the lane, and cross the stone bridge over the river Rye. Follow the cart track which bears right, with Ashberry Wood on your left. Ignore the signpost "Footpath

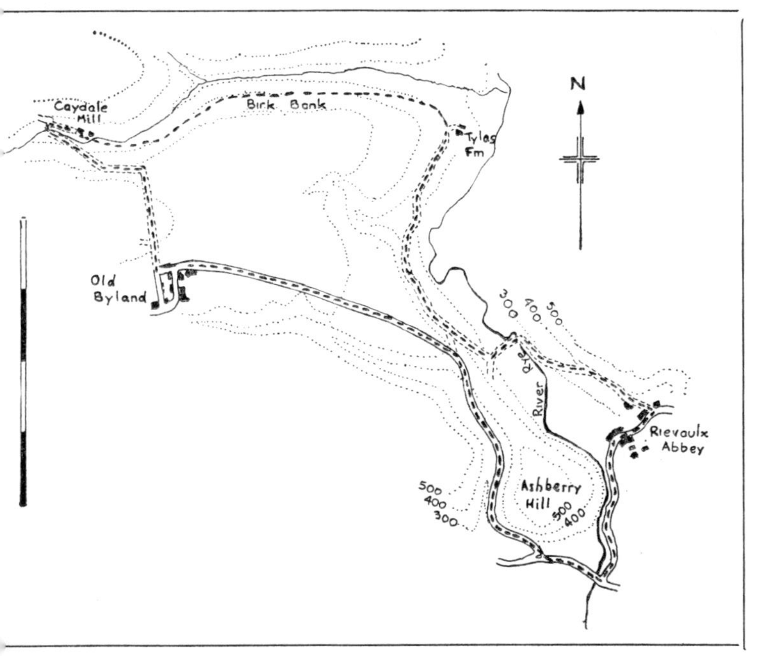

to Hawnby," since this is not very clear, and in due course keep right to follow the gated metalled road towards Tylas Farm. Where this bends right towards the farm, proceed through the gate ahead, and along a grassy track and over a stile into Birk Bank Wood. The path goes ahead through the wood and through several gates. Eventually a wall borders the path on the right and the stream can be heard below in the woods.

Caydale Mill comes into view. When the wall ends go through the mill yard and across a ford on to road from Old Byland to Murton. Keep Caydale Mill on your right. Turn left up steep incline on to the good road. Shortly turn left with the signpost, Rievaulx $2\frac{3}{4}$ miles. Follow this lane past the top of Old Byland village street, and follow the signs back to Rievaulx. Although this is a metalled road, it is possible to walk on the wide grass verges for most of the distance. After descending Ashberry Hill and passing Ashberry Farm on your left, turn left at the T-junction, and then immediately after crossing the river Rye turn left again to return to the car-park.

Distance : 6 miles.

ROPPA EDGE

Starting Point : Car park at the top of Newgate Bank on B1257 (Stokesley - Helmsley), G.R. 563890.

Public Transport : At the time of writing this walk is suitable for the non-motorist since the Middlesbrough - Helmsley Service 292 passes this point.

TAKE THE TRACK which trends in an easterly direction from the car park, signposted to Cow House Bank. After passing through a short stretch of forest the track emerges on to an open moor and follows the summit of the ridge, with a steep slope down on the left and a gentle slope over on the right. The view from this track is magnificent, since it embraces the Vale of Pickering and the Howardian Hills beyond on the right, and the excellent view up Bilsdale to Hasty Bank on the left. In two miles the ordnance point on the summit of the moor is reached and from this point, not only is there an excellent view of much of the western section of the Moors, but Buckden Pike and Great Whernside are clearly visible in the far west.

From the summit continue forward along the track, and where a metalled road comes in from the right pass through the gate opposite. Follow this track in a south-easterly direction to pass through some coniferous forest and reach the Helmsley - Bransdale road at the summit of Cow House Bank. Turn acute left, and descend the bank into Riccal-

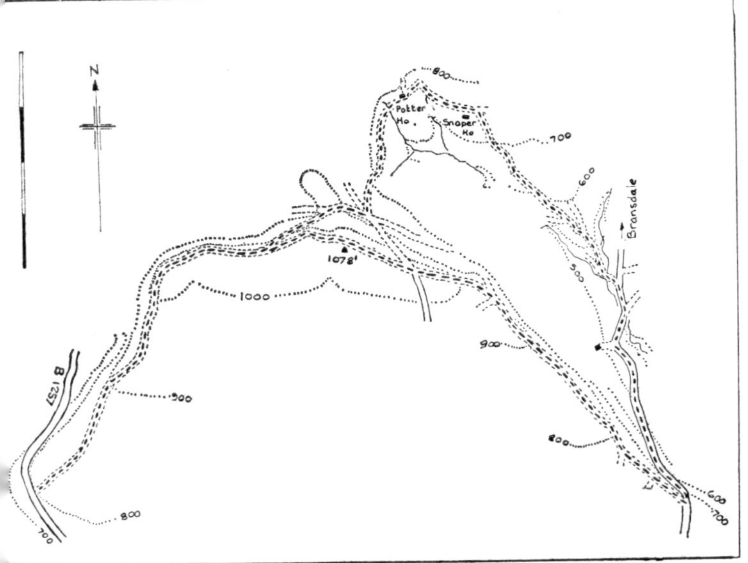

dale near the hamlet of Lund. In about three-quarters-of-a-mile take the track on the left which crosses Bogmire Gill and then bears right to enter the forest on Collins Ridge.

On entering the forest take the left fork, which starts by going north-of-west and bears gradually to the right to become a straight track going in a north-westerly direction. Turn left at the second cross-roads to emerge on to the open moor with farmland on the left. Pass the small farm of Snaper House on the left to reach the second farm, Potter House. Leave by the farm road which keeps the forest, Roppa Wood, on the right. At the foot of the escarpment there is a cross-road where the main track turns left to ascend the hill. Turn right here, and gradually ascend the escarpment to regain the outward track a quarter-of-a-mile west of the summit. Where the track emerges from the Roppa Wood take care to follow the left fork. On regaining the outward route follow it back to the cars.

Distance : 9 miles.

BRANSDALE AND FARNDALE

Starting Point: On the minor road from Fadmoor to Bransdale, where it makes a right-angle bend to descend into Bransdale. G.R. 659927.

START BY walking northwards along the Rudland Rigg road for about half-a-mile to where a cart-track cuts off to the right and goes to White House — a derelict farmhouse seen on the moors to your right. Turn along this track and continue to White House, where the track forks. Take the left fork and continue on for about a mile to where the cart-track ends just above the quarry. The footpath starts here, breaks back in a hairpin to skirt the quarry and then passes the workings on your left-hand as it drops down to the valley seen on your right. Follow the path down to its lowest point at a gate on your right. Go through the gate — it is wet here — and follow the path through a field and through a gate on to the minor road from Low Mill to Keysbeck. Cross the road to a cottage below and on to the main Gillamoor - Low Mill road.

Continue on the road down into Low Mill and turn left over the bridge. There is a litter-box on the corner of the car park here, and at this corner is a signpost "Footpath to Church Houses," pointing down a field. This footpath is the famous "Daffodil Walk." The stretch of footpath along the banks of the river Dove from Low Mill to Church Houses is known as "Daffodil Walk," since during every April this valley is a sea of daffodils. So many visitors come to this district that it is necessary for a one-day traffic system to pertain on Saturdays and Sundays during April. The Dale is permanently threatened by plans to flood most of its upper reaches to provide a reservoir to supply water to Hull and Sheffield.

Opposition against such a scheme is organised through the Farndale Defence Committee, a joint committee representing local interests, the Ramblers' Association and C.P.R.E.

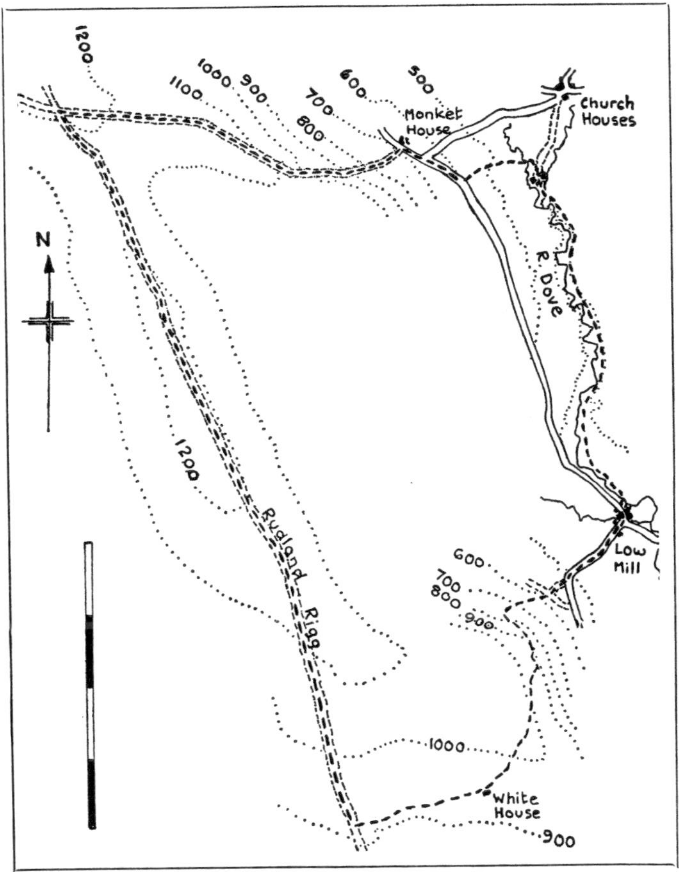

Follow the path right through the valley until a derelict mill, High Mill, is reached. Pass in front of the adjacent occupied cottages, and follow the farm-track for a few yards to where it passes through two gates before carrying on to Church Houses. Your path, however, is over a small bridge across the beck on your left before you reach the second gate. Climb up the bank to the road at the top, then pass through a gate on to the road and turn right (there is a signpost pointing the way you have come, and stating "to High Mill").

Continue straight on past the right-hand fork to Church Houses, on to the road which follows the west side of the dale to the final limits of habitation. Immediately after passing the farm on the right (Monket House), there is a gate on your left with a sign which says "Unsuitable for Motors." Go through this gate and climb up the hill and over the moor; there are some old quarry workings on your left and a broken railing on your right, where at some stage large rocks have come down the hillside. Have no fear; they have been like this since the second world war. Continue on this track until it meets another one at right-angles, and turn left along this new track. This is Rutland Rigg again and you can follow it right down to the start of the walk where you have parked the car.

Distance : 10 miles.

UPPER FARNDALE

Starting Point : Summit of Blakey Ridge, half-a-mile to the south of "The Lion Inn." G.R. 684989.

START BY walking along the old railway track in a north-westerly direction, following the signpost, "Footpath to Bloworth," about twenty yards on the right along the lane sign-posted to Farndale. The track keeps level round the head of Blakey Gill, and after a mile-and-a-quarter enters a shallow cutting. At the far end of the cutting, a narrow track ascends the side to the left. This track should be followed

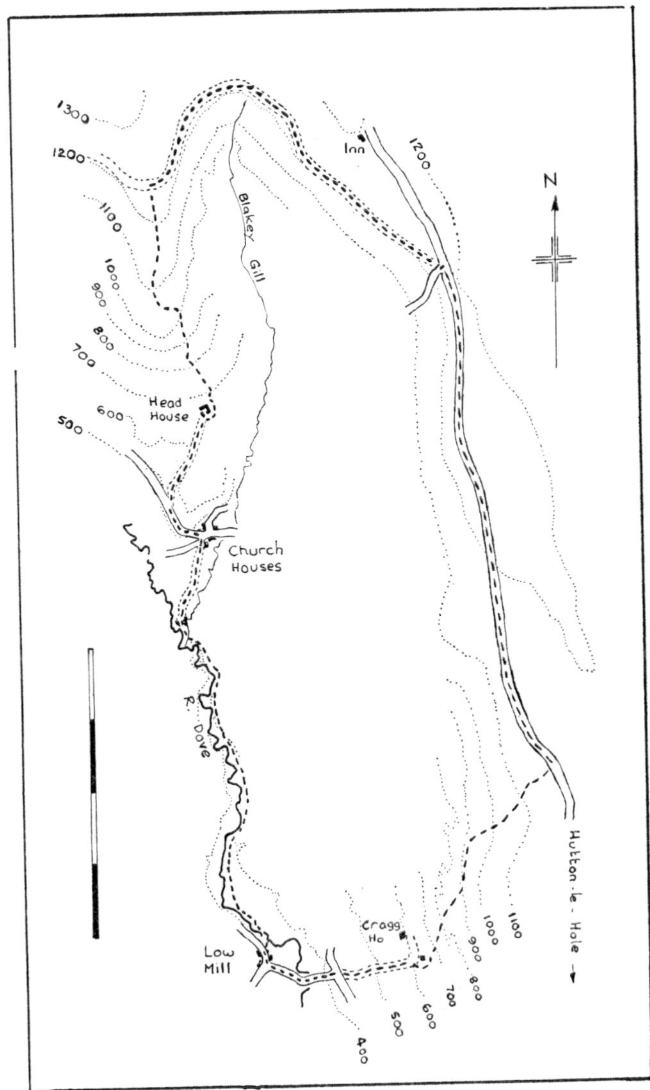

There is no designated right-of-way on the path running north from Church Houses parallel to Blakey Gill.

along the summit of the ridge between Blakey Gill and Farndale, towards a prominent cairn which should be passed on the right.

Beyond the cairn, the track which is known as Jackson's Road descends to the left, and after passing below a short escarpment goes through a gate. Proceed downhill towards Head House Farm, not far ahead and surrounded by oak trees. Pass through another gate, and then pass the oak trees on your right to go through a farm gate with the farm on your right. Keep the farm buildings on your right to join the access road which descends into Farndale (the right of way is by Hall Farm).

On joining the metalled road, turn left into the hamlet of Church Houses. The lane finishes at a T-junction in front of the local hostelry, the Feversham Arms, and your way should be along the lane immediately to the right of that building. The lane soon reaches the banks of the little river Dove, and after passing through High Mill becomes a footpath which follows the left bank of the river down to Low Mill. This is the famous Daffodil Walk which is a sea of daffodils every April. In a mile-and-a-half from Church Houses a substantial footbridge across the river Dove, immediately below the village of Low Mill, is reached. Cross the bridge and ascend to reach the lane on the outskirts of that village.

Turn left to enter the village, and at the road junction in the centre turn left to descend back to the valley bottom and ultimately to reach a T-junction of metalled roads. Opposite is a gate through which you should pass to ascend the daleside — a hedge, beyond which is a cricket ground, is on your right. On reaching some ruins pass through a gate on the right, and follow the track as it winds round to the left and ascends the hillside diagonally with the dale on your left. On reaching the moor strike directly across to reach the main Hutton-le-Hole - Castleton road. Turn left along this road to reach the starting point in two miles.

Distance : 8 miles.

LOCKTON MOOR CIRCULAR

See map on page 60.

Starting Point: Saltergate on the Whitby-Pickering road (A169) at G.R. 853937, adjacent to the A.A. phone box.

Public Transport: United Service 91 (Whitby-Pickering-Malton) operates along this road.

TAKE THE ROAD from the north end of the car park signposted "Foot Path to Crosscliffe." At Newgate Foot continue straight on along the cart track into the woods. At a Y-junction take the right fork to pass the Bride Stones and reach Low Staindale. On reaching the valley bottom do not cross the stream, but turn right (west) to reach Low Pasture House. Take the farm road from here past Whitethorn Farm to reach the T-junction by High House. Turn right here and follow this track across Grime Moor back to Newgate Foot, from where you return to the car park via the outward route.

Distance: 7 miles.

LOWER ROSEDALE

Starting Point: At Bank Top on the Hutton-le-Hole to Rosedale Abbey road near to the site of the former Rosedale Chimney. G.R. 723947.

COMMENCE THE WALK by descending the Rosedale Bank along the road in a northerly direction. At the foot of the hill, at the cross-roads by an inn, turn right immediately beyond the inn to follow a narrow road along the right-hand side of the valley. The road gradually deteriorates as it passes a series of farms, and ultimately reaches the last one, Hollins Farm, after crossing a small stream. Keep all the

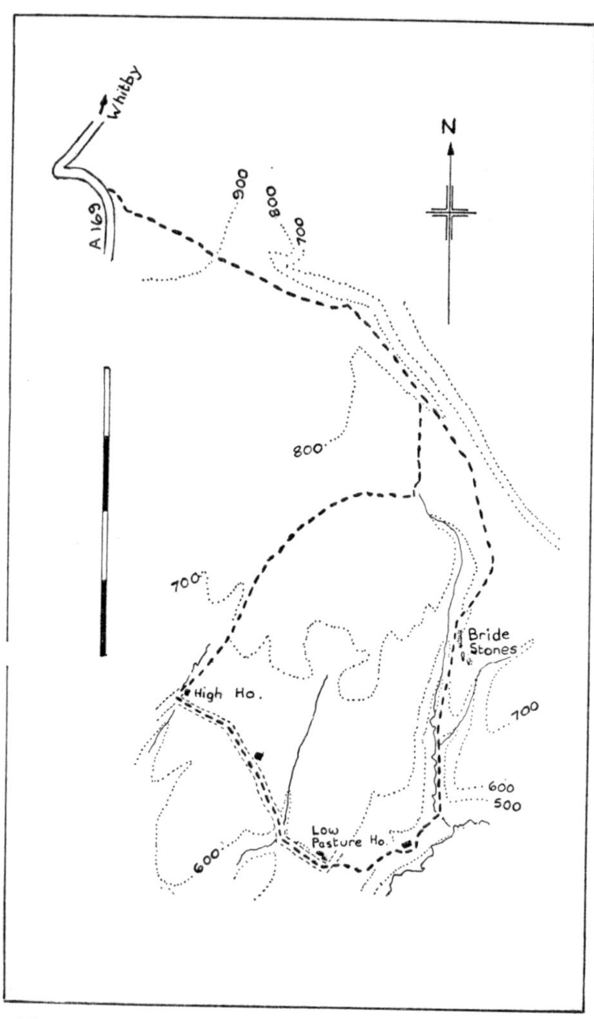

The recommended route is to the east of the Bride Stones.

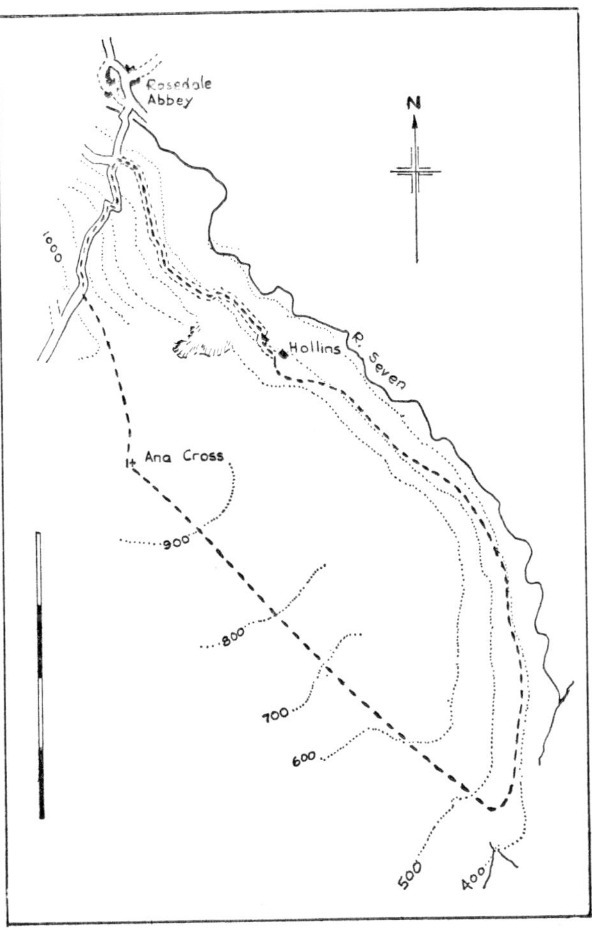

farm buildings on your left and the route will continue to be distinct, now taking the form of a broad track with a stone-wall on your left marking the boundary between the uncultivated moor on your right and the intake on your left.

Follow this track along the valley bottom until you are three-and-a-half miles from the cross-roads, and have passed the entrance to Hartoft Dale on the opposite bank. At this point leave the track by turning right over the moor, and after ascending for about half-a-mile you will reach another broad track. Turn right along this track, and follow it to return to the cars in a further three miles, passing Tranmire Plain and Ana Cross on the way.

(N.B.: Most of the western portion of this walk is not a definitive right of way).

Distance: 8 miles.

UPPER ROSEDALE

Starting Point: At Bank Top on the Hutton-le-Hole to Rosedale Abbey road near to the site of the former Rosedale Chimney. G.R. 723947.

COMMENCE THE WALK by descending the Rosedale Bank along the road in a northerly direction. At the foot of the hill, at the cross-roads by an inn, turn left along a narrow metalled road along the west side of the dale. In a mile-and-a-quarter, just before an acute left-hand bend is reached, turn right down a short farm road to Thorgill Farm. Pass between the farm buildings and cross the River Seven, and then ascend gradually through the fields to the terrace of cottages above. These cottages are extremely conspicuous, since they do not blend effectively with the surrounding countryside, but rather appear as if they had been transferred bodily from one of the central areas of Hull or Middlesbrough. They were built originally for workers in the old mining industry.

On reaching the lane take the track which ascends the dale side immediately opposite, and in another quarter-of-a-mile the old mine workings at the end of the old railway will have been reached. Turn left here, and from now on the route is straight forward along the railway track for seven miles back to the car park around the head of the valley.

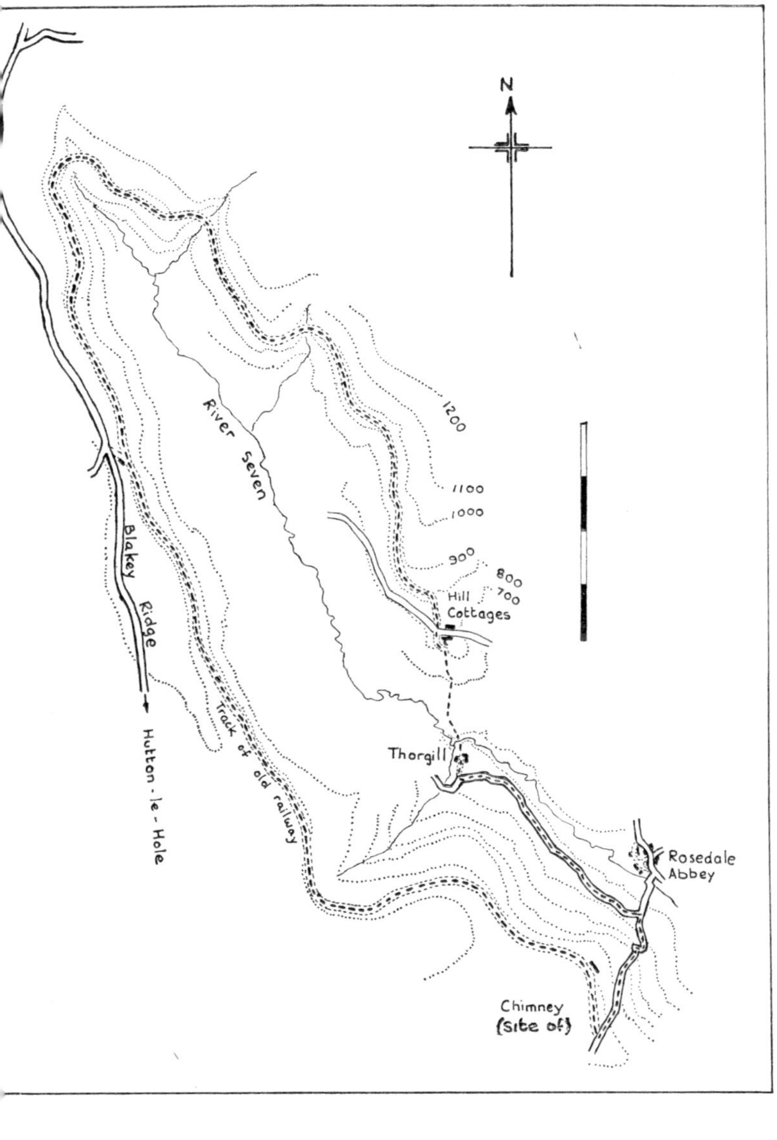
N
River Seven
1200
1100
1000
900
800
700
Hill
Cottages
Blakey
Ridge
Hutton-le-Hole
Track of old railway
Thorgill
Rosedale
Abbey
Chimney
(site of)

Distance: 10 miles. Note:—We understand that the old railway track is not officially designated as a right-of-way, but at the same time we believe that the farmers and tenants in Rosedale prefer walkers to use the railway rather than the cultivated fields.

LEVISHAM MOOR CIRCULAR

Starting Point: Adjacent to the A.A. phone box on the Whitby-Pickering road (A169) near Saltergate. G.R. 853937.

Public Transport: United Service 91 (Whitby-Pickering-Malton) operates along this road.

FROM THE CAR PARK proceed in a northerly direction away from Pickering to reach the angle of the hair-pin bend in a quarter-of-a-mile. From this point go through a gate and walk in a westerly direction on top of a ridge along a cart track, passing Seavy Pond on your right to reach Dundale Pond (a pleasant place for a picnic) in two miles.

From Dundale Pond take the track down the valley due east to reach Levisham Beck. Cross the beck and walk in a north-easterly direction between the beck and the wall. Do not go through the adjacent gate. Keep climbing slightly until you reach the wood on your right, from where you should continue to walk in a north-easterly direction through the fields to Low Horcum Farm. From here, take the cart track which leads past High Horcum Farm back to the hair-pin bend, from where you return to the car park via the Main Road.

An extension from Dundale Pond is to continue along the track from Saltergate for an additional quarter-of-a-mile, and then to pass through a gate on your left to reach a rough road which leads down to Levisham village. Turn left by the inn and post office to follow another rough road back to the tributary valley below Dundale Pond.

Distance: $4\frac{1}{2}$ miles (extension to Levisham, 2 miles).